T0061520

ISBN 978-1-4768-6781-6

HAL•LEONARD®
CORPORATION
7777 W. BLUEMOUND RD. P.O. BOX 13819 MILWAUKEE, WI 53213

In Australia Contact:
Hal Leonard Australia Pty. Ltd.
4 Lentara Court
Cheltenham, Victoria, 3192 Australia
Email: ausadmin@halleonard.com.au

Visit Hal Leonard Online at
www.halleonard.com

CONTENTS

4   **TEENAGE DREAM**

9   **LAST FRIDAY NIGHT [T.G.I.F.]**

15   **CALIFORNIA GURLS** FEAT. **SNOOP DOGG**

19   **FIREWORK**

26   **PEACOCK**

31   **CIRCLE THE DRAIN**

35   **THE ONE THAT GOT AWAY**

40   **E.T.**

44   **WHO AM I LIVING FOR?**

48   **PEARL**

54   **HUMMINGBIRD HEARTBEAT**

59   **NOT LIKE THE MOVIES**

TEENAGE DREAM

Words and Music by KATY PERRY,
BONNIE McKEE, LUKASZ GOTTWALD,
MAX MARTIN and BENJAMIN LEVIN

Moderate Dance beat

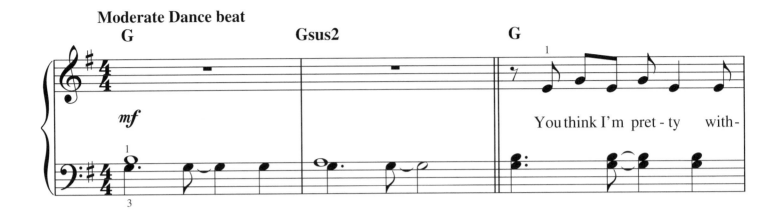

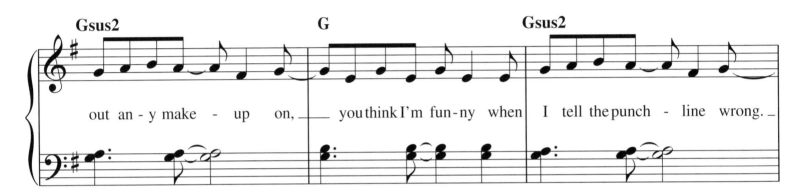

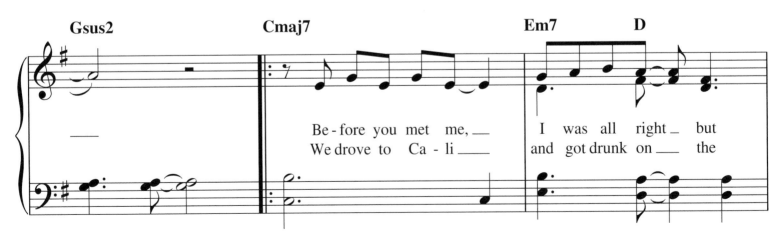

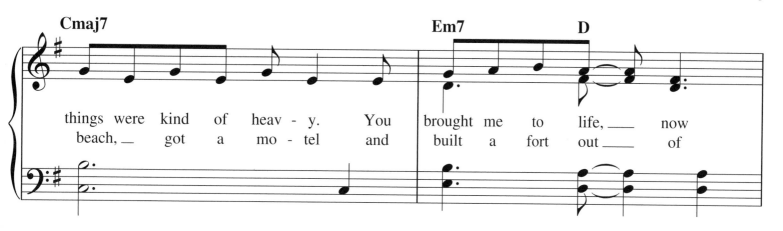

Cmaj7

Em7 **D**

things were kind of heav - y. You brought me to life, ___ now
beach, __ got a mo - tel and built a fort out ___ of

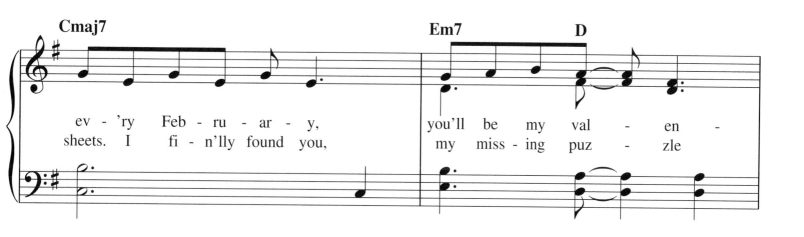

Cmaj7

Em7 **D**

ev - 'ry Feb - ru - ar - y, you'll be my val - en -
sheets. I fi - n'lly found you, my miss - ing puz - zle

Cmaj7

Em **Dsus** **D** **Cmaj7**

tine, _____ val - en - tine. _____ Let's go all the way __
piece. _____ I'm com - plete. _____

Em **D** **Cmaj7**

Em **Dsus** **D**

___ to - night; no re - grets, just love. ___ We can

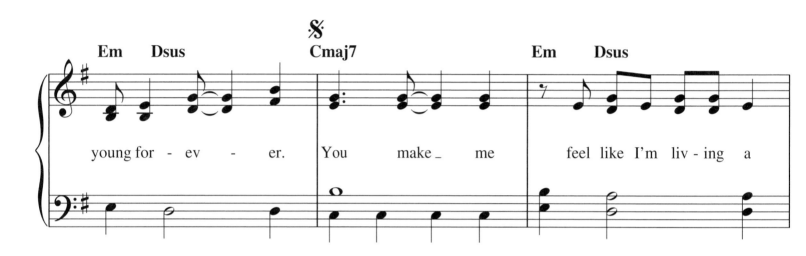

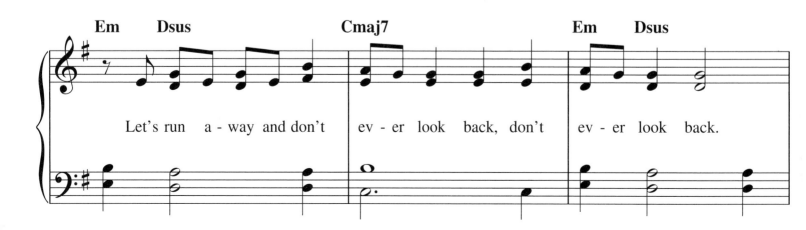

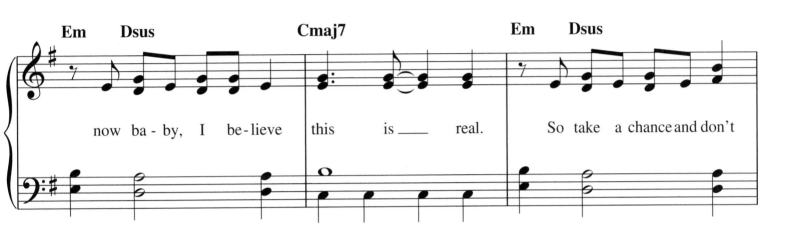

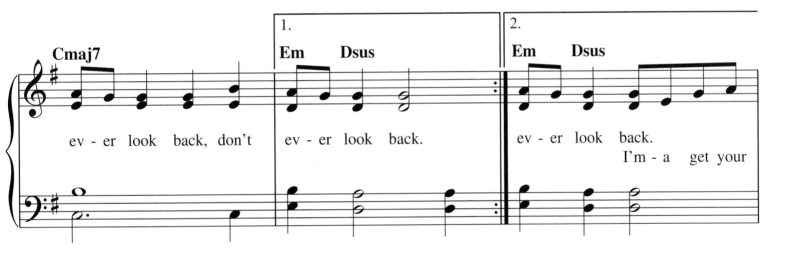

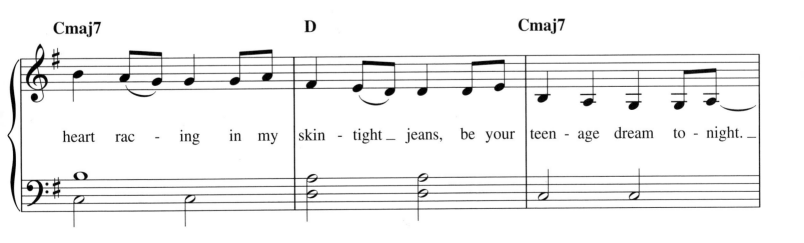

Let you put your hands on __ me in my skin - tight _ jeans, be your

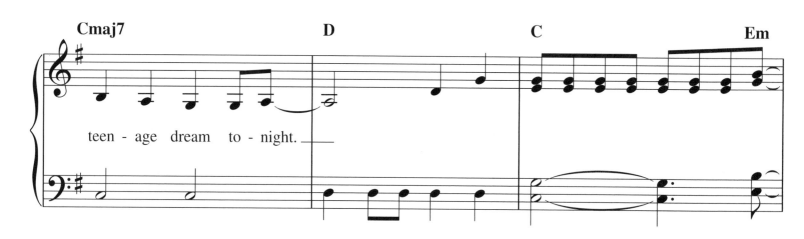

teen - age dream to - night. ___

teen - age dream to - night. ___

LAST FRIDAY NIGHT
(T.G.I.F.)

Words and Music by KATY PERRY,
BONNIE McKEE, LUKASZ GOTTWALD,
MAX MARTIN and BENJAMIN LEVIN

With energy

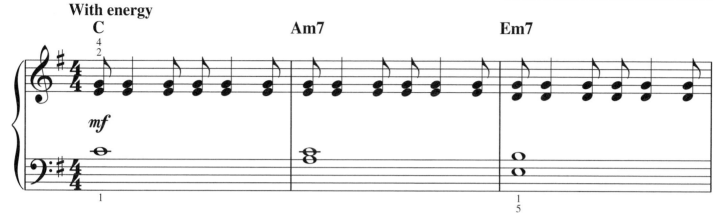

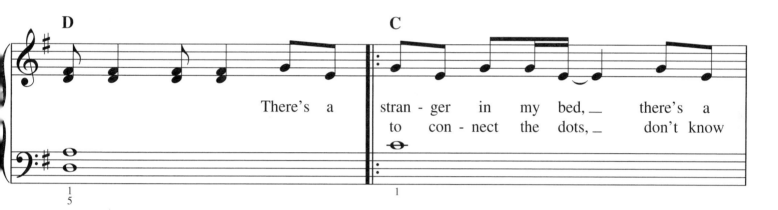

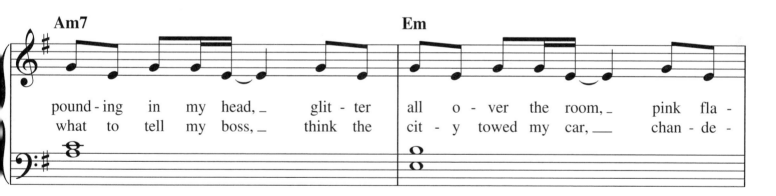

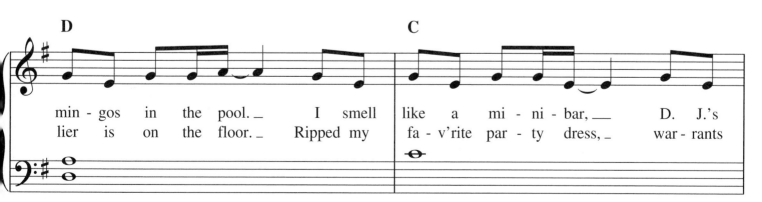

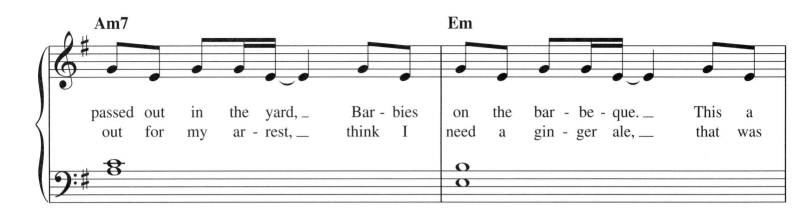

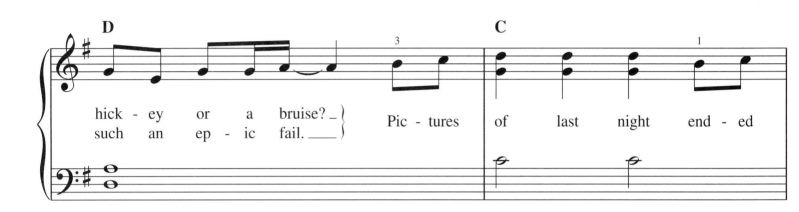

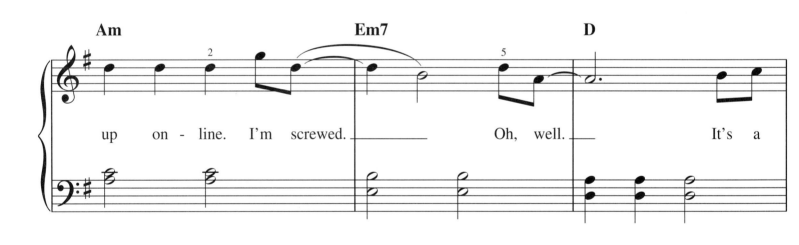

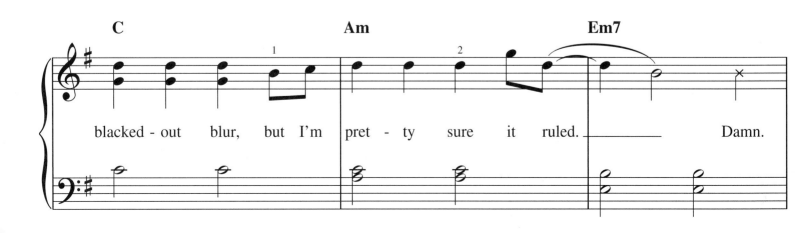

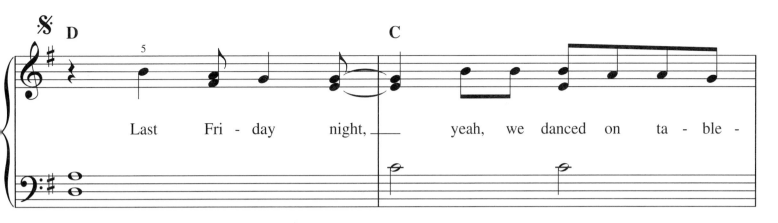

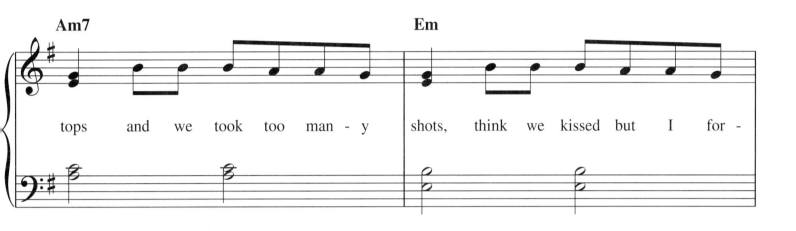

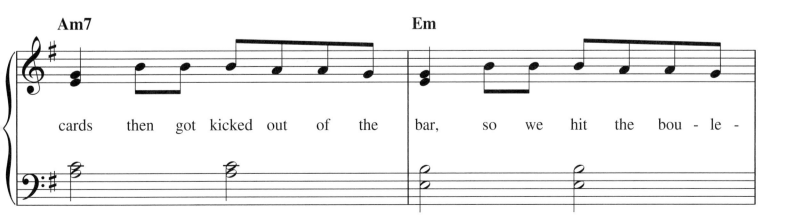

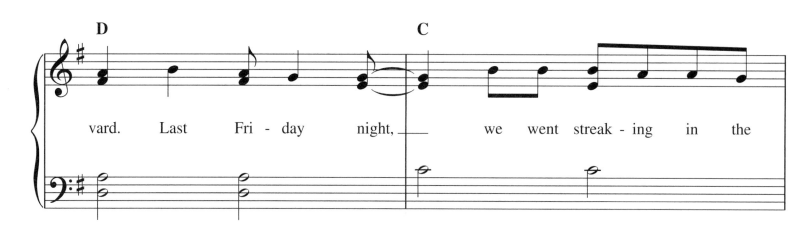

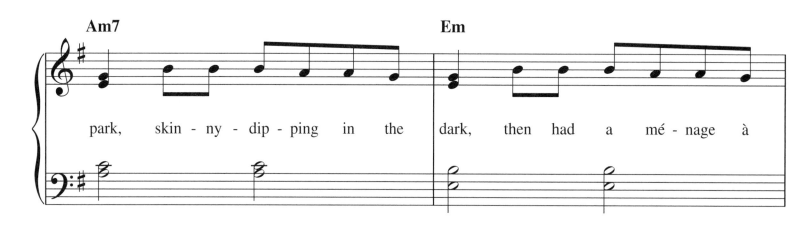

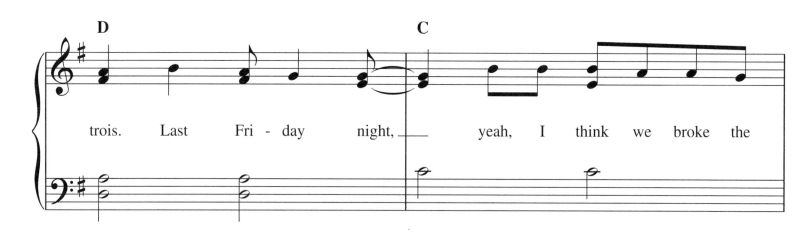

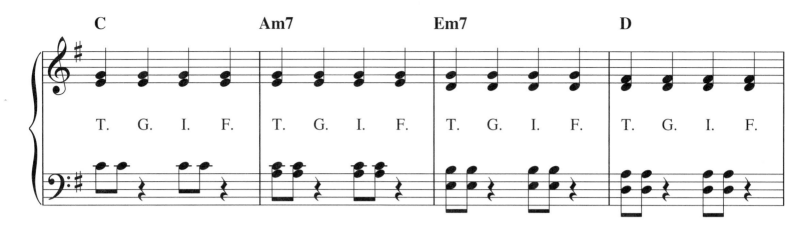

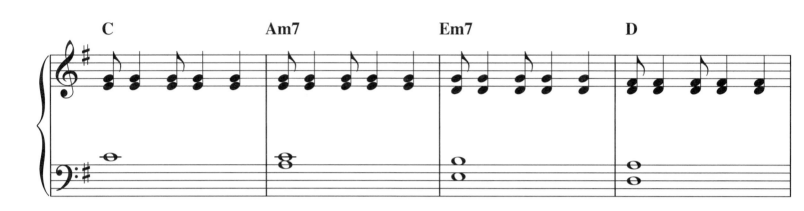

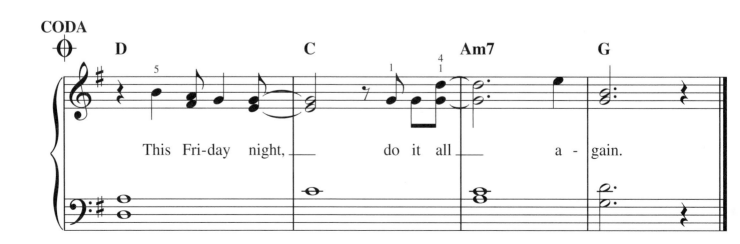

CALIFORNIA GURLS

Words and Music by KATY PERRY,
BONNIE McKEE, LUKASZ GOTTWALD,
MAX MARTIN, BENJAMIN LEVIN,
and CALVIN BROADUS

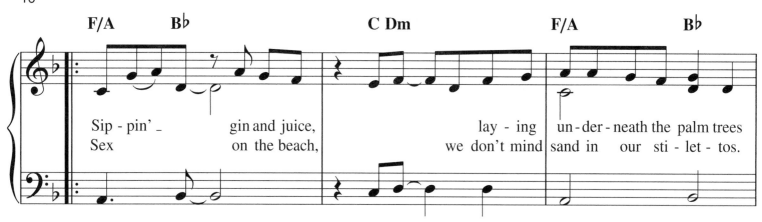

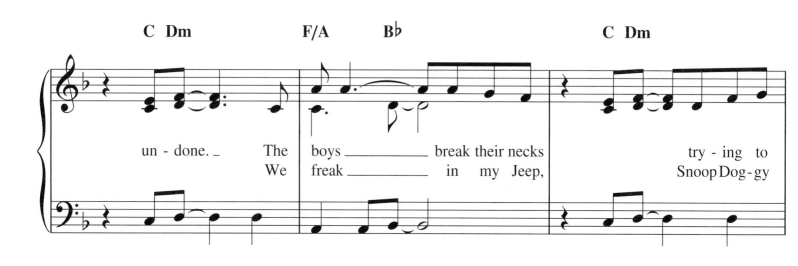

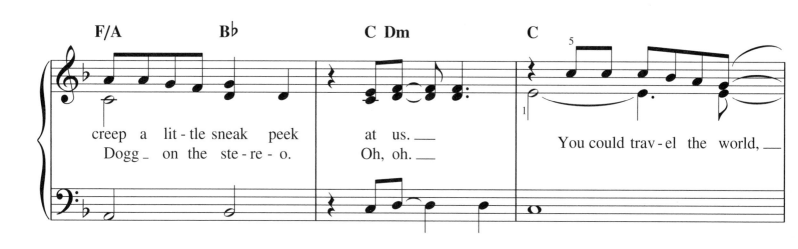

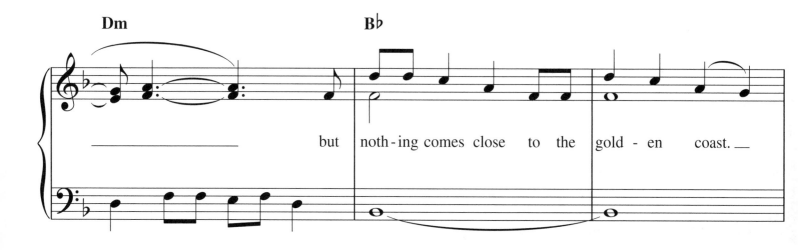

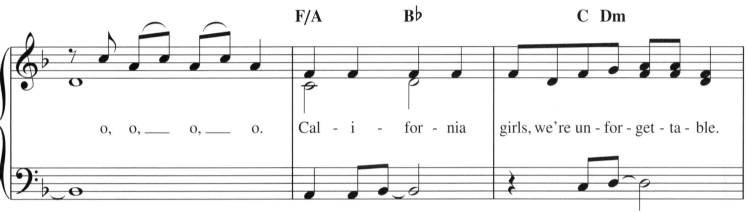

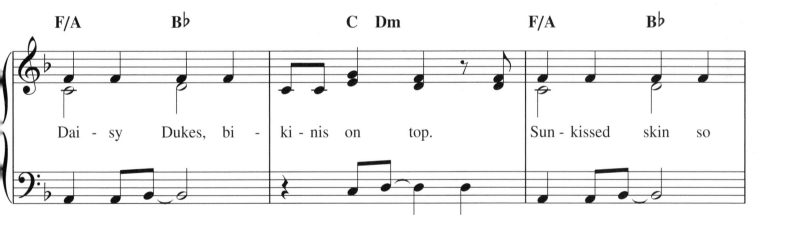

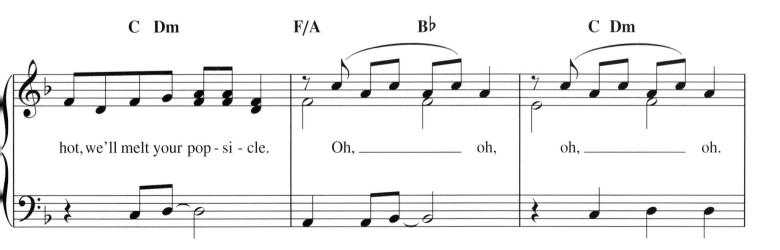

Cal - i - for - nia girls, we're un-de-ni-a-ble. Fine, fresh, fierce, we

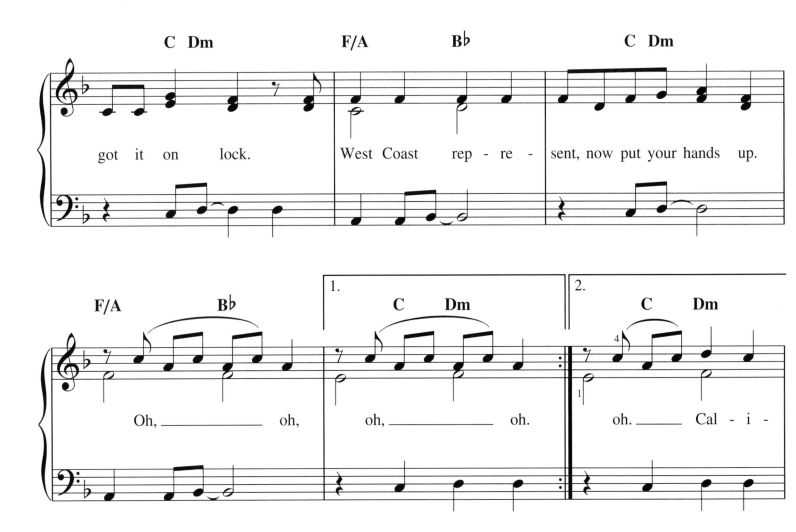

got it on lock. West Coast rep - re - sent, now put your hands up.

Oh, _____ oh, oh, _____ oh. oh. _____ Cal - i -

for - nia __ girls.

FIREWORK

Words and Music by KATY PERRY,
MIKKEL ERIKSEN, TOR ERIK HERMANSEN,
ESTHER DEAN and SANDY WILHELM

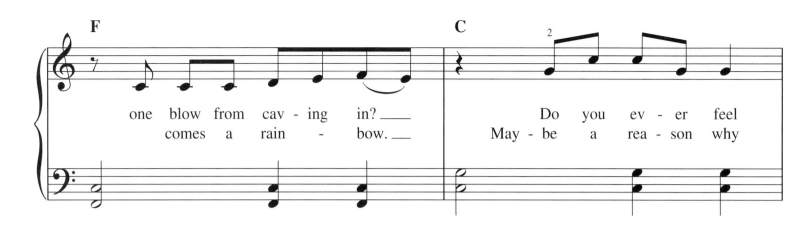

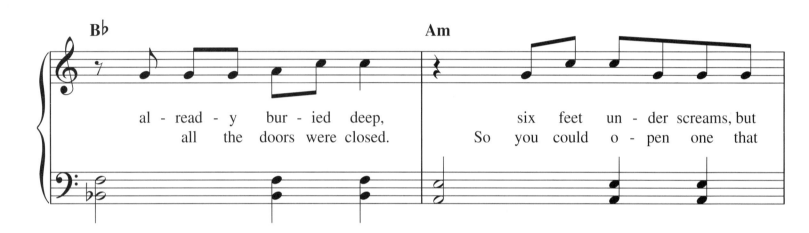

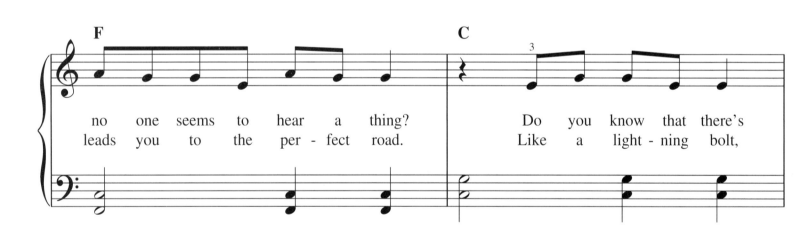

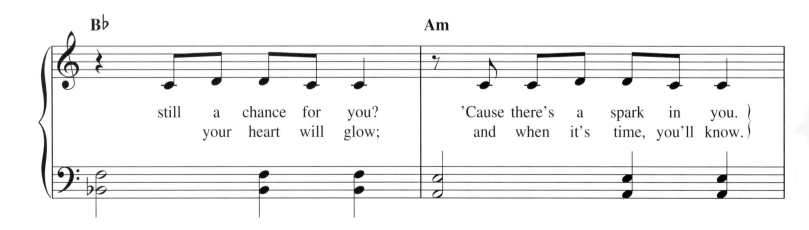

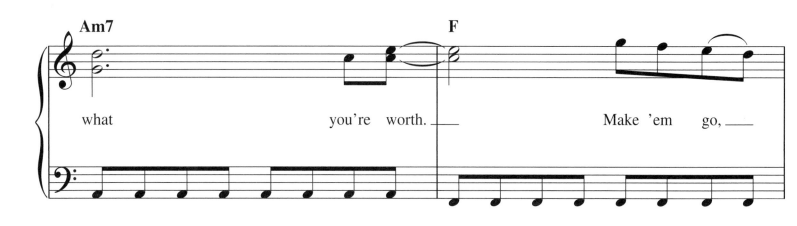

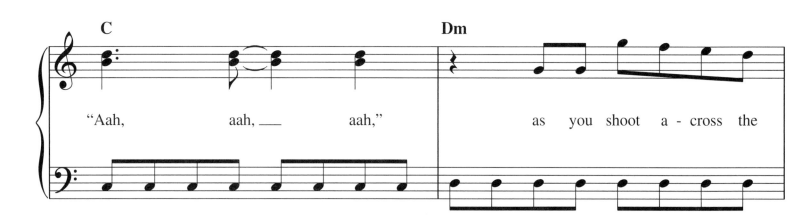

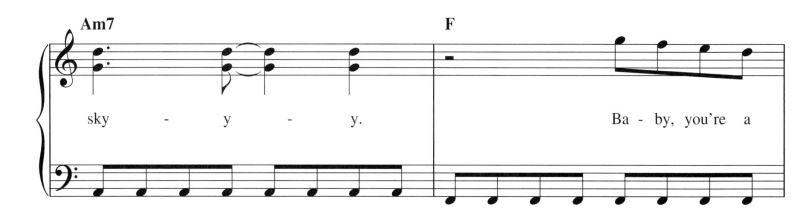

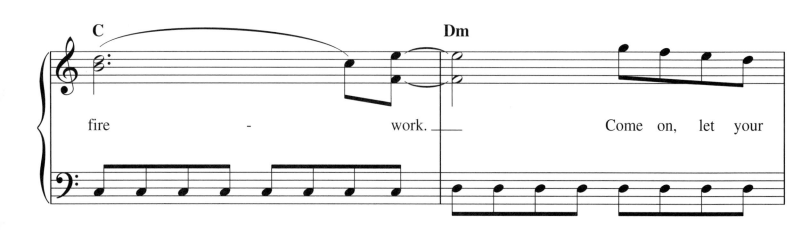

col - ors burst. ___ Make 'em go, ___

"Aah, aah, ___ aah," you're gon - na leave 'em all in

awe, awe, ___ awe. ___

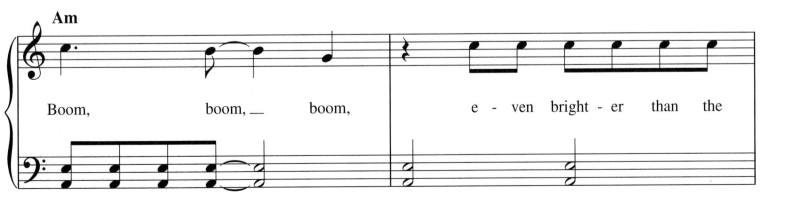

Boom, boom, ___ boom, e - ven bright - er than the

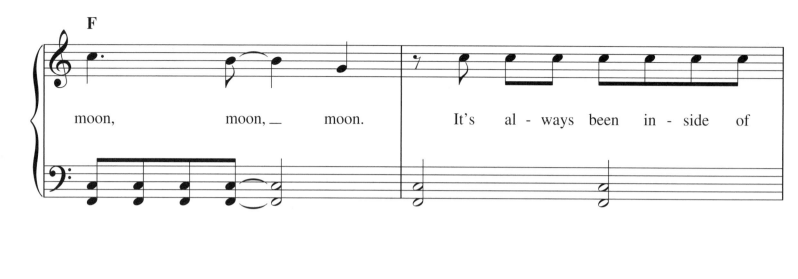

moon,   moon,   moon.   It's al - ways been in - side of

you,   you,   you,   and now it's time to let it

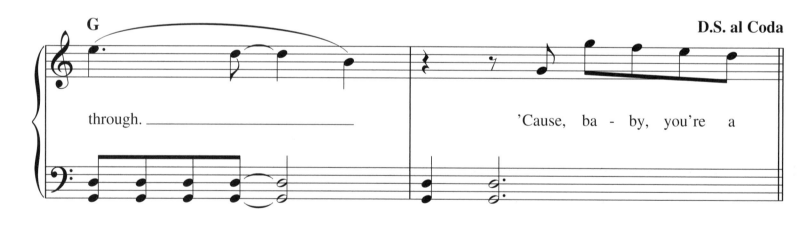

through. _____   'Cause, ba - by, you're a

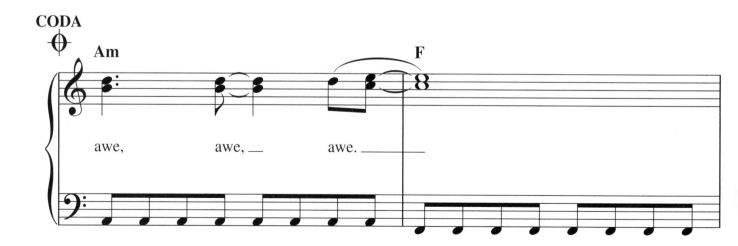

awe,   awe, __   awe. _____

C Boom, boom, boom, **Dm** e - ven bright - er than the

Am moon, moon, moon. **F**

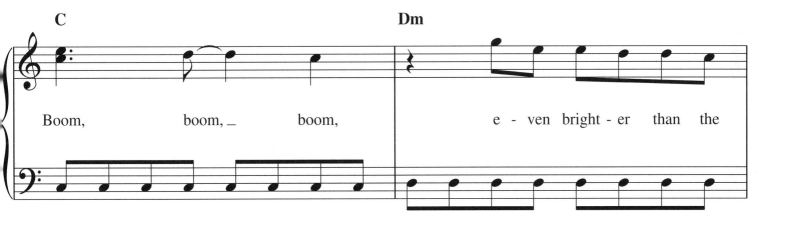

C Boom, boom, boom, **Dm** e - ven bright - er than the

Am moon, moon, moon. **F**

PEACOCK

Words and Music by KATY PERRY,
MIKKEL ERIKSEN, TOR ERIK HERMANSEN
and ESTHER DEAN

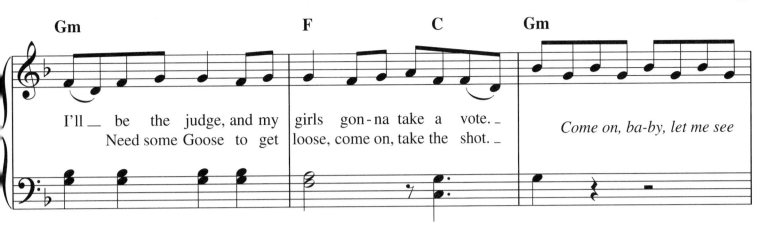

I'll __ be the judge, and my girls gon-na take a vote. __
Need some Goose to get loose, come on, take the shot. __
Come on, ba-by, let me see

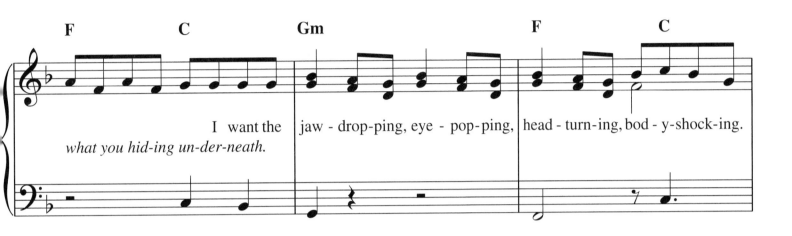

what you hid-ing un-der-neath.
I want the jaw - drop-ping, eye - pop-ping, head - turn-ing, bod - y-shock-ing.

Oh, oh, _____ oh, oh, oh. __ I want my heart throb-bing, ground shak-ing,

show stop-ping a - maz-ing. Oh, oh, _____ oh, oh, oh, _____

Are you brave e-nough to let me see your pea - cock? Don't be a chick-en, boy; stop

act - ing like a bee - otch. I'm - a peace out if you don't give me the pay - off.

Come on, ba - by, let me see what you hid-ing un - der - neath. Are you brave e - nough to

let me see your pea - cock? What - cha wait-ing for? It's time for you to show it off.

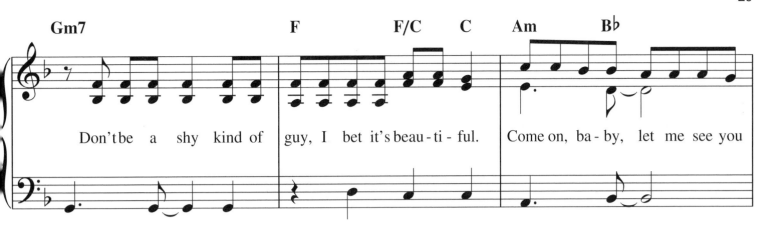

Don't be a shy kind of guy, I bet it's beau-ti-ful. Come on, ba-by, let me see you

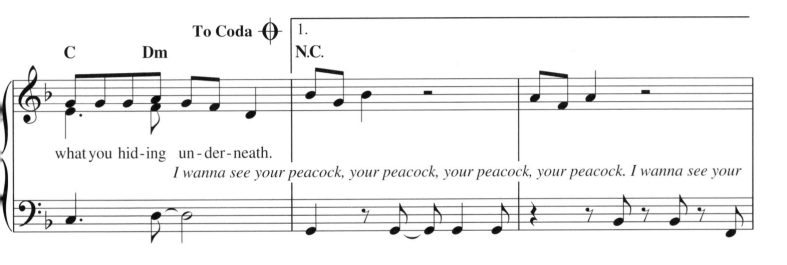

To Coda ⊕

1.

N.C.

what you hid-ing un-der-neath.

I wanna see your peacock, your peacock, your peacock, your peacock. I wanna see your

2.

Gm

peacock, your peacock. *peacock, your peacock.* *peacock, your peacock,*

your peacock, your peacock.

Oh, my God, no ex - ag - ger -
You got the fin - est ar - chi -

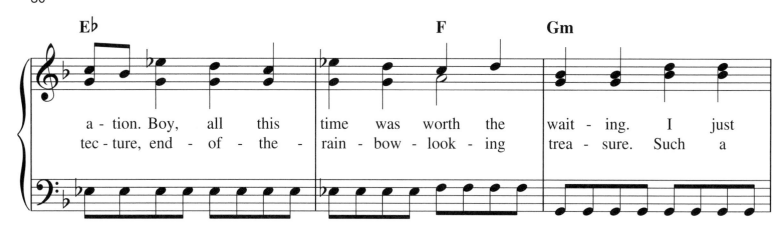

a - tion. Boy, all this time was worth the wait - ing. I just
tec - ture, end - of - the - rain - bow - look - ing trea - sure. Such a

shed a tear. I am so un - pre - pared.
sight to see, and it's all for me.

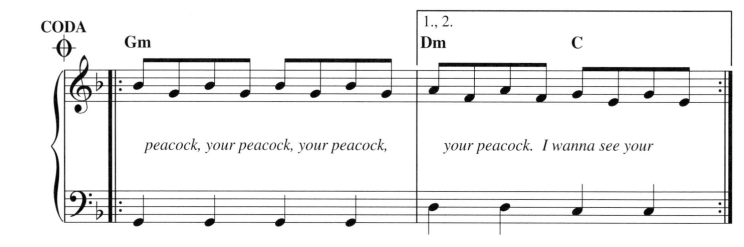

peacock, your peacock, your peacock, your peacock. I wanna see your

your peacock. Come on, ba - by, let me see what you hid - ing un - der - neath.

CIRCLE THE DRAIN

Words and Music by KATY PERRY,
CHRISTOPHER STEWART and LAMONT NEUBLE

why, ___ and say you're real - ly gon - na try. ___ If I had a
roll, ___ but you're real - ly just a joke. ___ Had the

nick - el for ev - 'ry time, I'd own the bank, bank, bank, bank. ___
world in the palm __ of your hand, but you cho - o - o - oked. ___

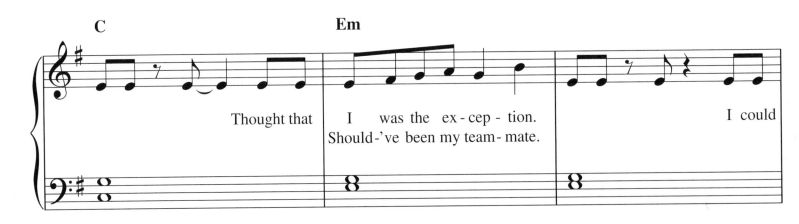

Thought that I was the ex - cep - tion. I could
Should-'ve been my team - mate.

re - write your ad - dic - tion. You could have been the great - est
Could-'ve changed _ your fate. You say ___ that you love me,

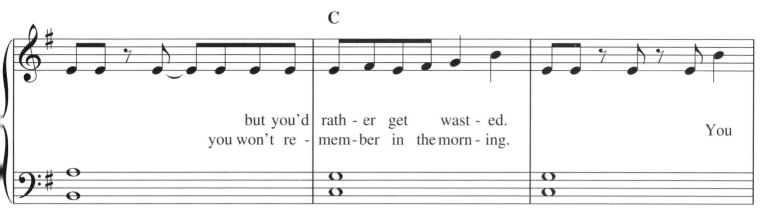

but you'd rath - er get wast - ed.
you won't re - mem - ber in the morn - ing.

You

fall a - sleep dur - ing fore - play 'cause the pills you take are

more your for - té. I'm not stick - ing a - round to watch _ you

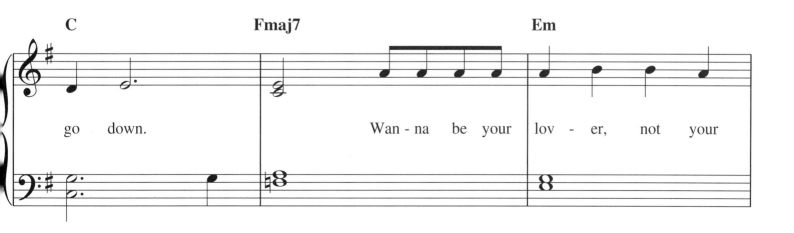

go down. Wan - na be your lov - er, not your

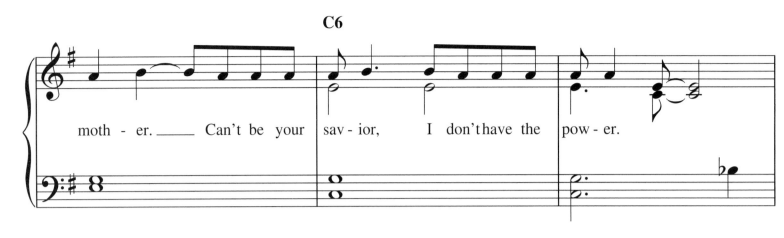

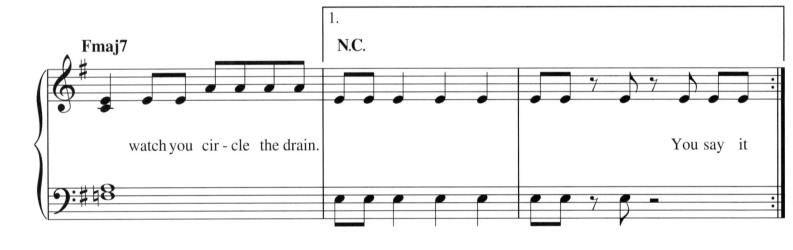

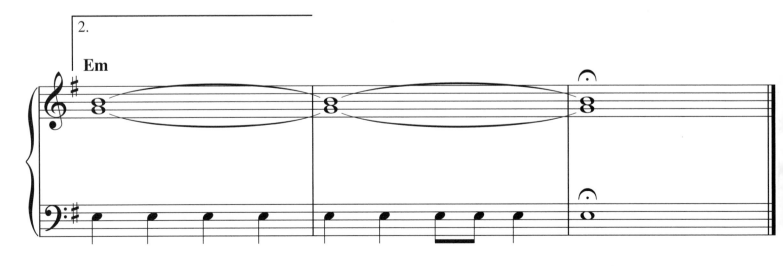

THE ONE THAT GOT AWAY

Words and Music by KATY PERRY,
MAX MARTIN and LUKASZ GOTTWALD

Bright Rock

Sum-mer af-ter high school, when we first met, ___ we'd
I was June and you were my John-ny Cash. ___ Nev-er

make out in your Mus-tang to Ra-di-o-head. ___ And
one with-out the oth-er; we made a pact. ___

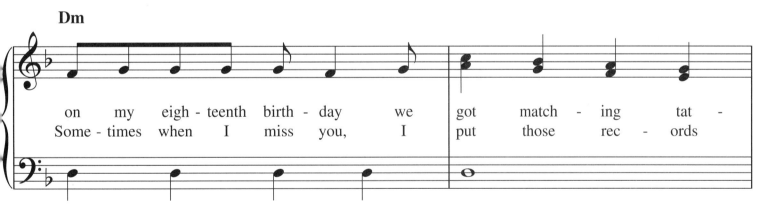

on my eigh-teenth birth-day we got match-ing tat-
Some-times when I miss you, I put those rec-ords

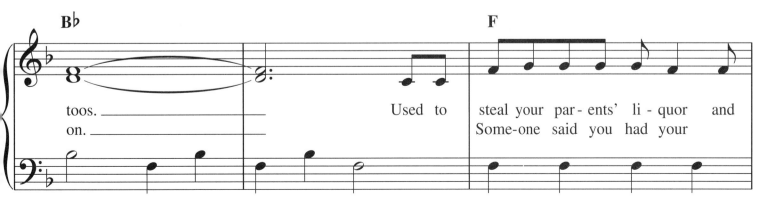

toos. ___ Used to steal your par-ents' li-quor and
on. ___ Some-one said you had your

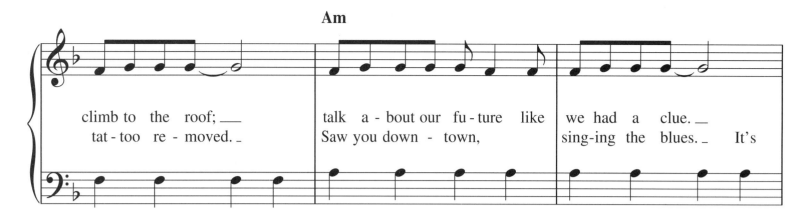

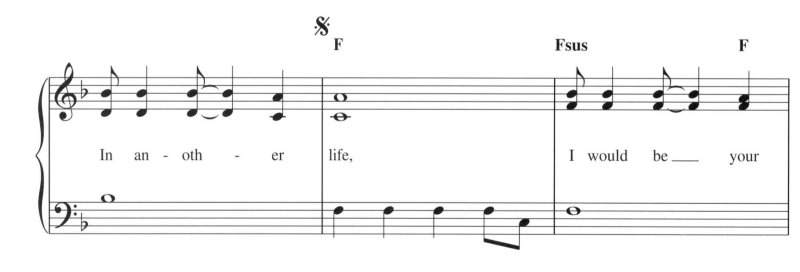

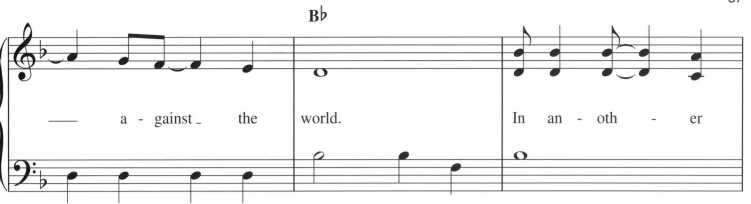

_____ a - gainst _ the world. In an - oth - er

life, I would make _ you stay, so

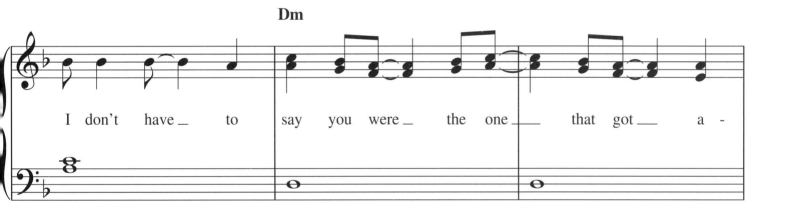

I don't have _ to say you were _ the one _ that got _ a -

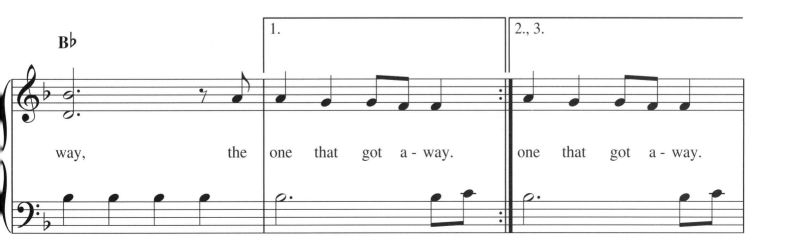

way, the one that got a - way. one that got a - way.

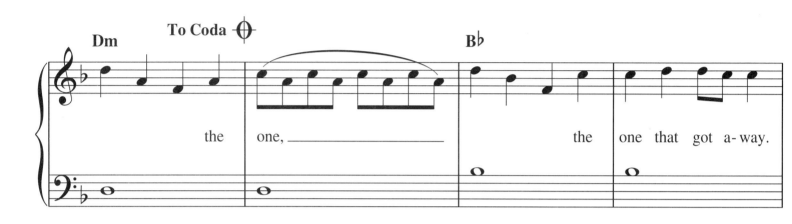

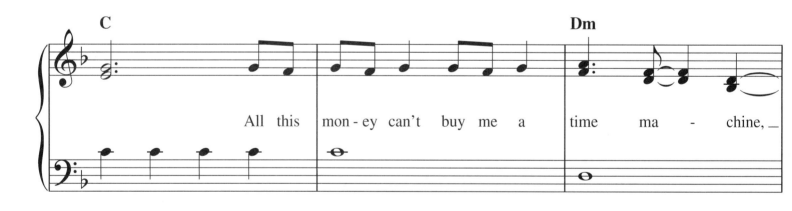

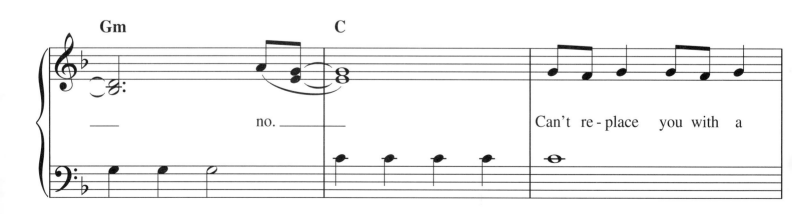

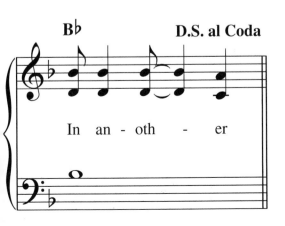

E.T.

Words and Music by KATY PERRY,
LUKASZ GOTTWALD, MAX MARTIN
and JOSHUA COLEMAN

whole 'noth - er world, a dif - f'rent di - men - sion. You

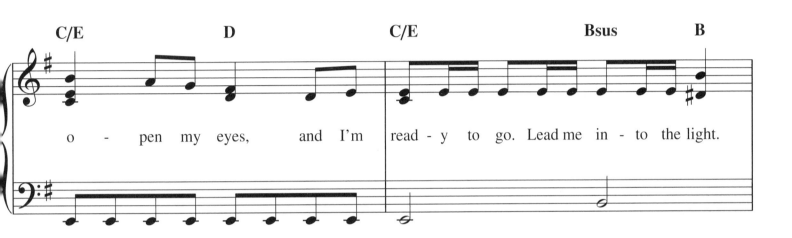

o - pen my eyes, and I'm read - y to go. Lead me in - to the light.

Kiss me, K - k - kiss me, in - fect me with your lov - ing, fill me with your poi - son.

Take me, ta - ta - take me. Wan - na be your vic - tim, read - y for ab - duc - tion.

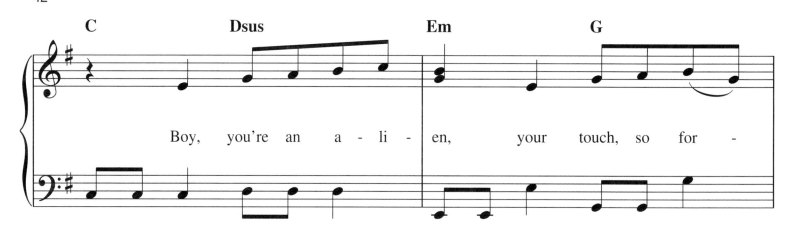

Boy, you're an a - li - en, your touch, so for -

To Coda

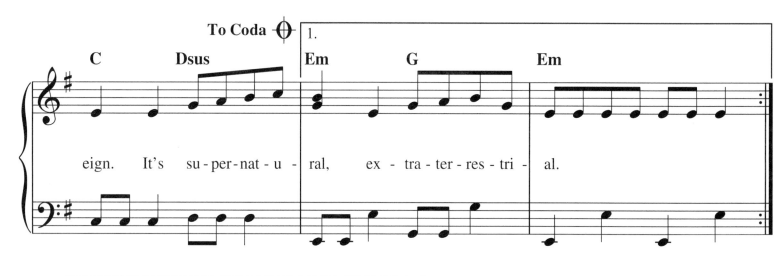

eign. It's su - per - nat - u - ral, ex - tra - ter - res - tri - al.

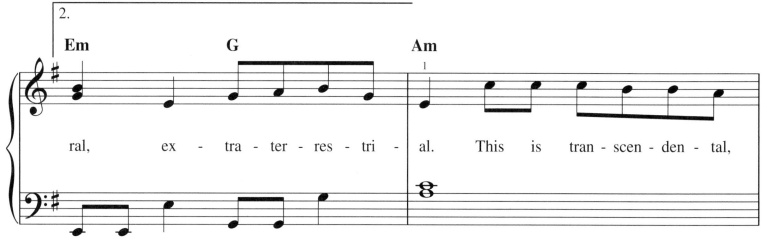

ral, ex - tra - ter - res - tri - al. This is tran - scen - den - tal,

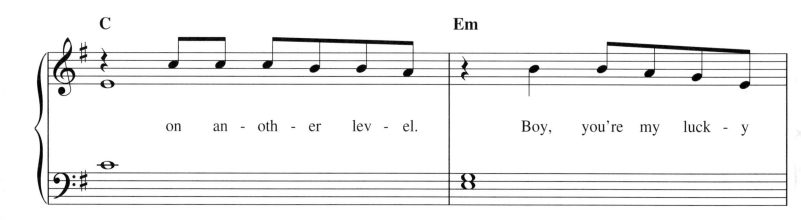

on an - oth - er lev - el. Boy, you're my luck - y

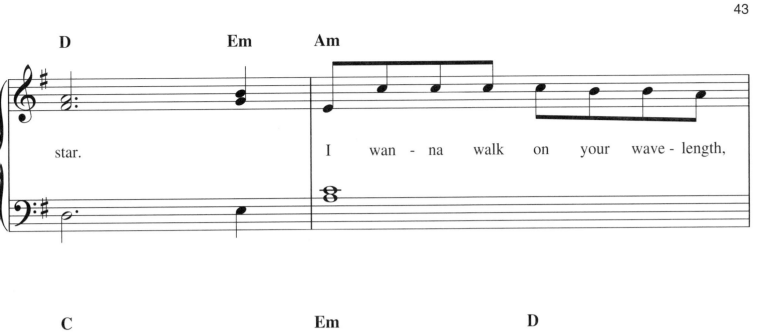

star.

I wan - na walk on your wave - length,

and be there when you vi - brate.

For you, I'll risk it all.

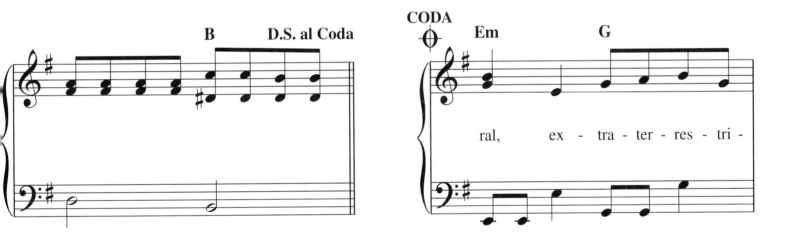

ral, ex - tra - ter - res - tri -

al.

Ex - tra - ter - res - tri - al.

WHO AM I LIVING FOR?

Words and Music by KATY PERRY,
CHRISTOPHER STEWART, BRIAN THOMAS
and LAMONT NEUBLE

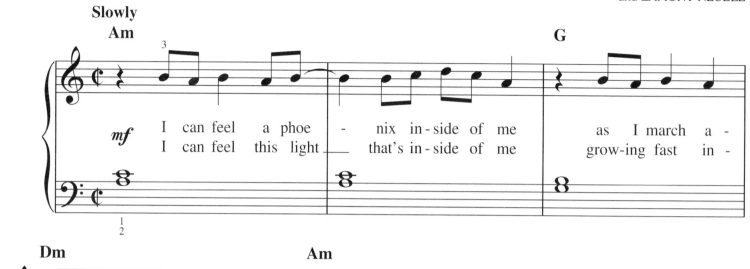

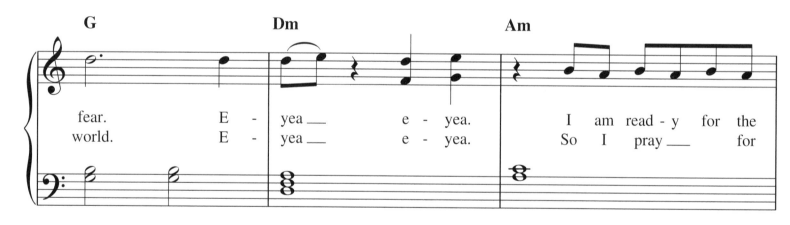

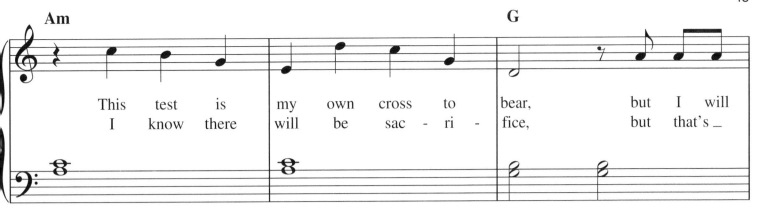

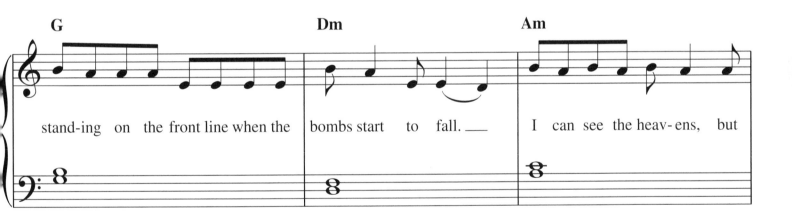

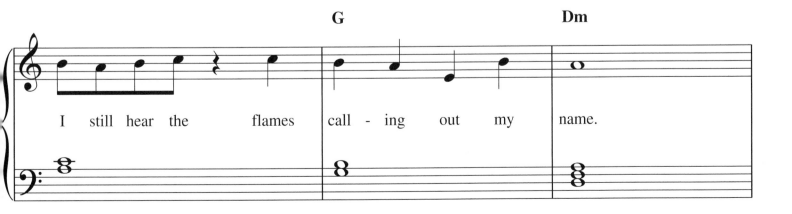

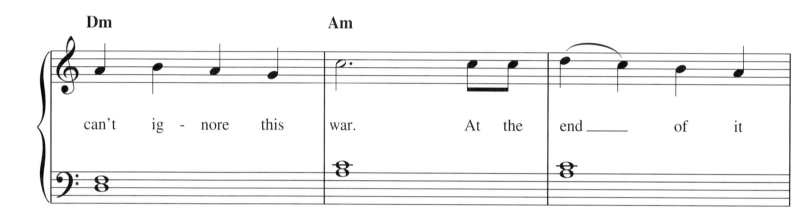

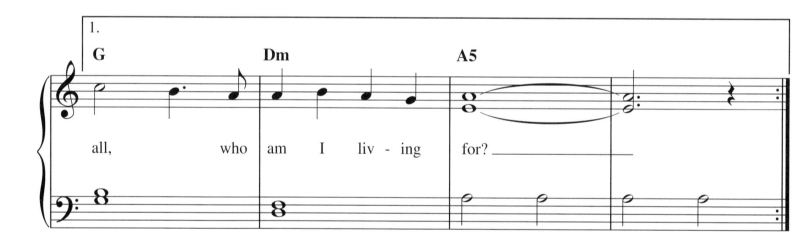

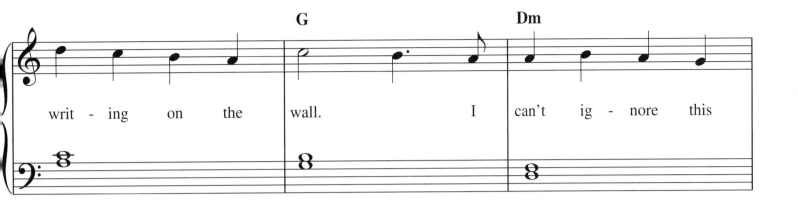

writ - ing   on   the   wall.   I   can't   ig - nore   this

war.   At   the   end ____ of   it   all,   who

am   I   liv - ing   for? __

At   the   end,   who   am   I   liv - ing   for? __

PEARL

Words and Music by KATY PERRY,
CHRISTOPHER STEWART and GREG WELLS

Moderately

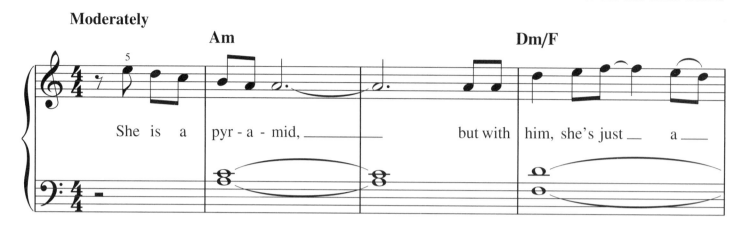

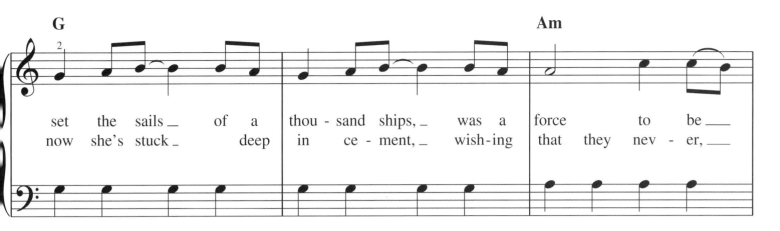

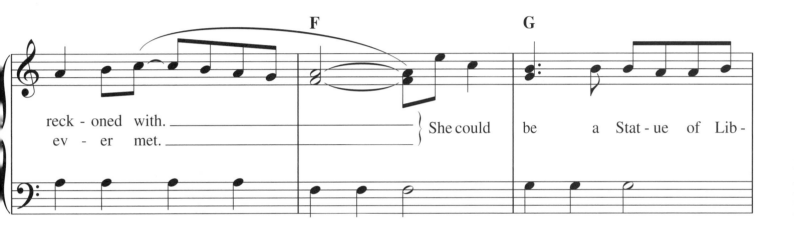

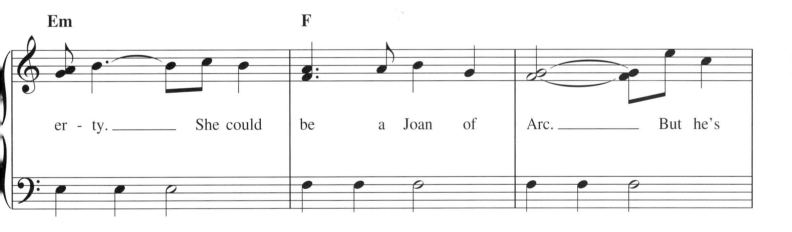

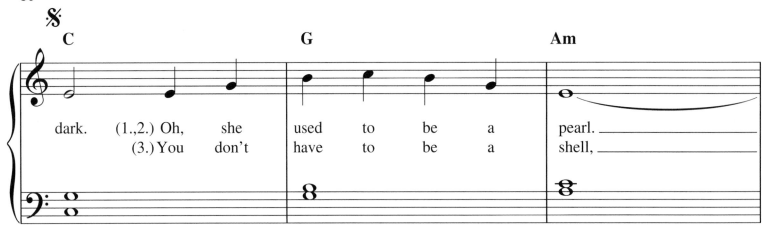

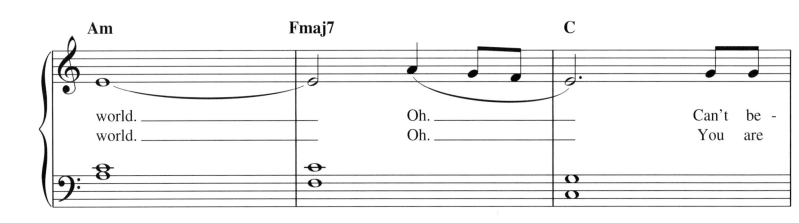

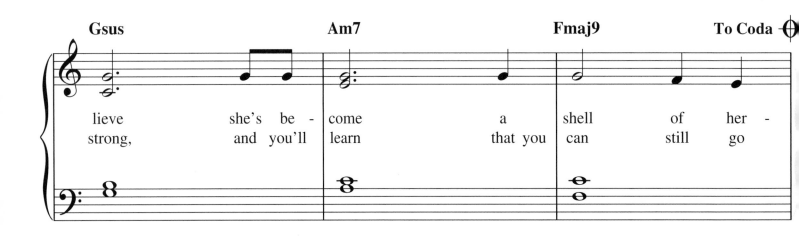

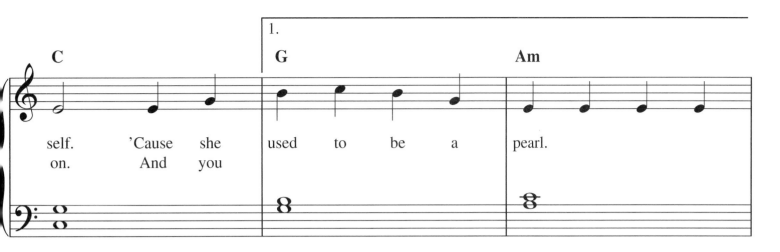

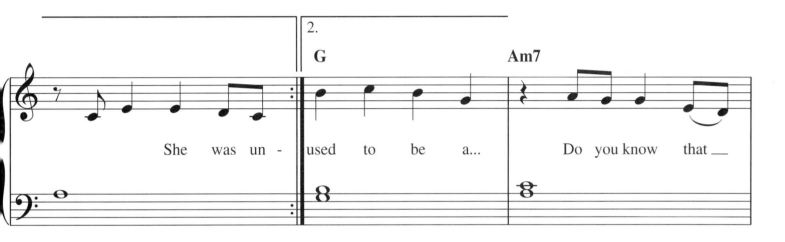

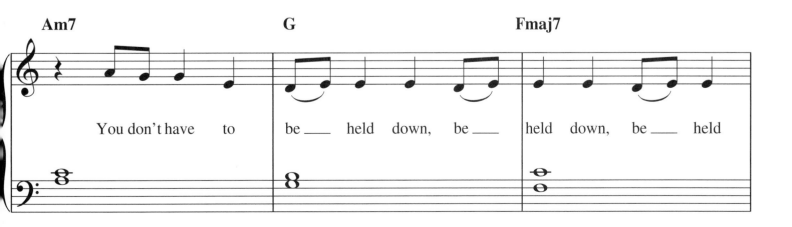

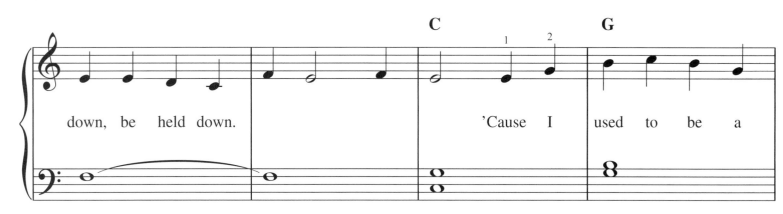

down, be held down. 'Cause I used to be a

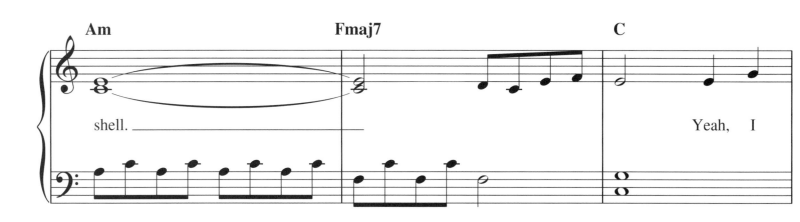

shell. Yeah, I

let him rule my world, my world. Oh, _____ yeah.

But I woke up and grew strong, and

I can still go on. ___ And no one can take my pearl. ___

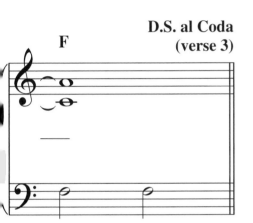

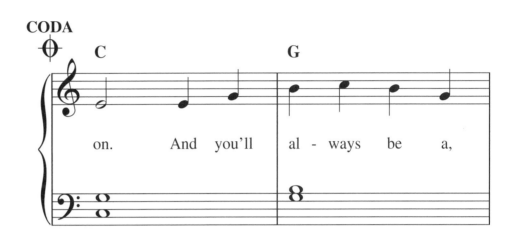

D.S. al Coda
(verse 3)

CODA

on. And you'll al - ways be a,

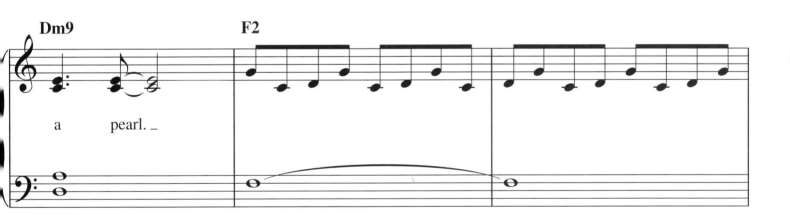

a pearl. ___

She is un - stop - pa - ble.

HUMMINGBIRD HEARTBEAT

Words and Music by KATY PERRY,
CHRISTOPHER STEWART, STACY BARTHE
and LAMONT NEUBLE

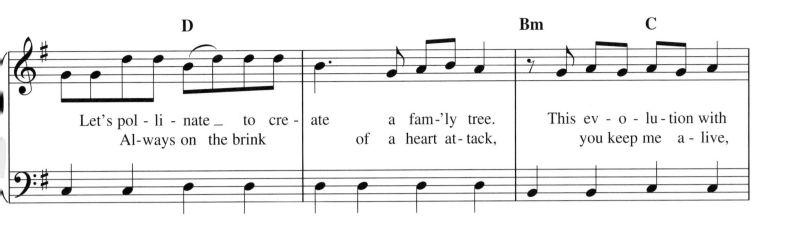

56

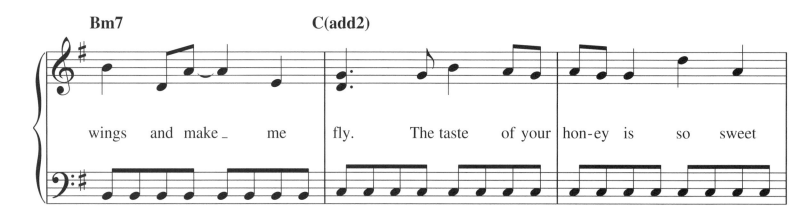

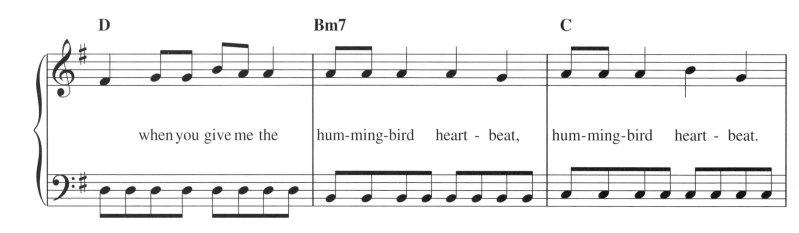

To Coda ⊕

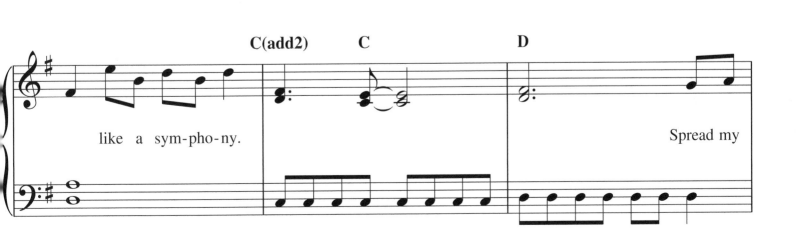

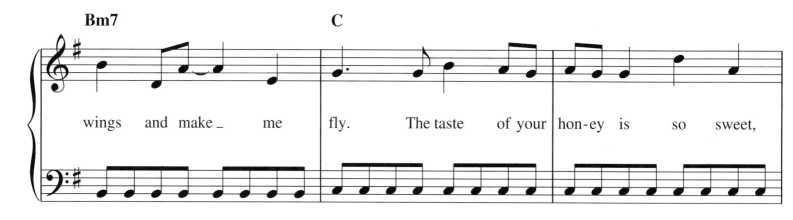

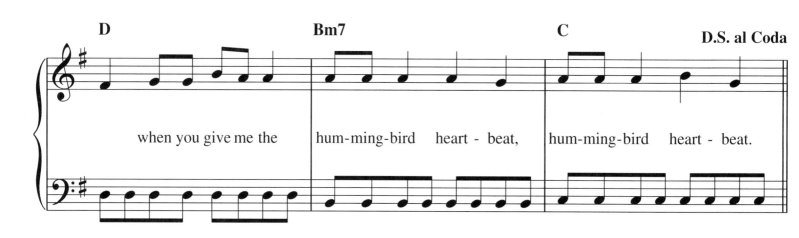

NOT LIKE THE MOVIES

Words and Music by KATY PERRY
and GREG WELLS

Moderately

He put it on me, I put it on, _____ like there was noth-ing
Snow White said when I was young, "One day my prince will

wrong. It did-n't fit, it was-n't right, _____ was-n't just the
come." _ So _____ I wait for that date. _

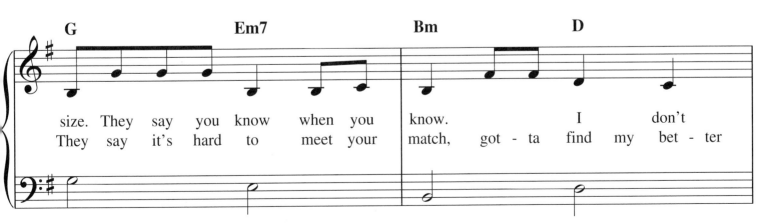

size. They say you know when you know. I don't
They say it's hard to meet your match, got-ta find my bet-ter

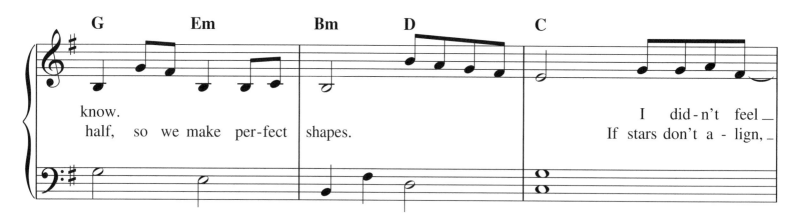

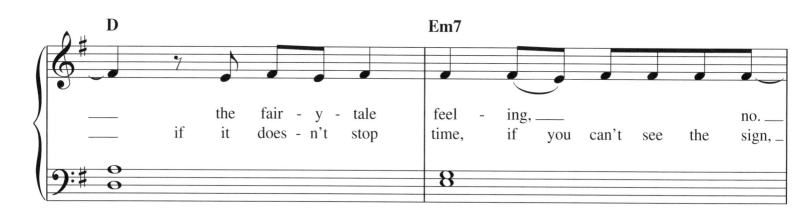

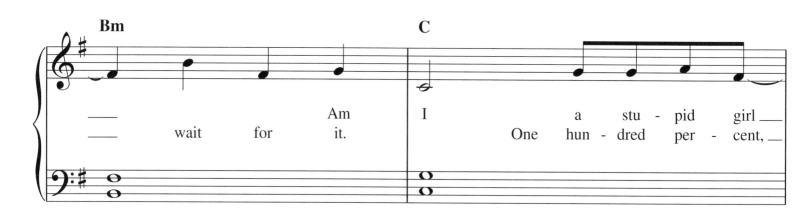

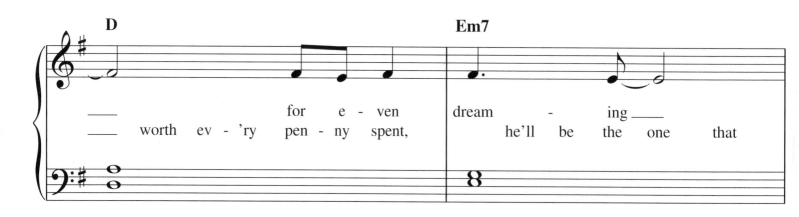

- gin- ing.

Oh, __ oh, _____ yeah. 'Cause I know you're out there. And you're,

mf

you're look- ing for me, oh. _____ It's a cra - zy i-

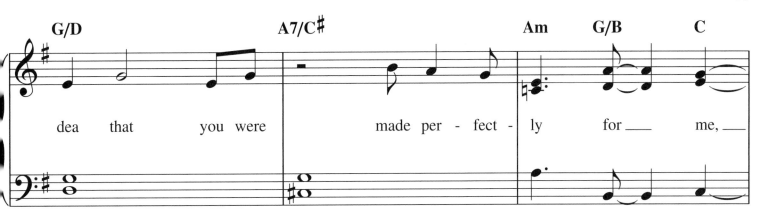

dea that you were made per - fect - ly for ___ me, ___

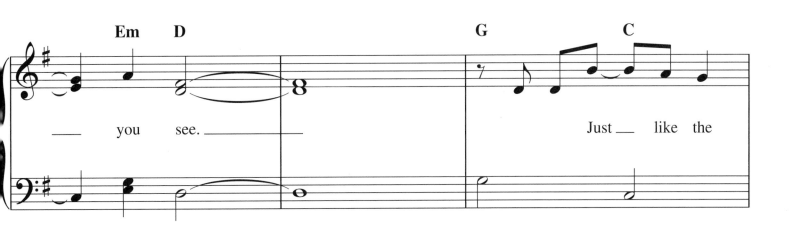

___ you see. ___ Just ___ like the

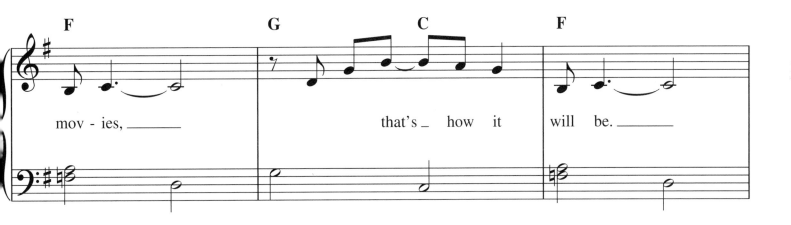

mov - ies, ___ that's ___ how it will be. ___

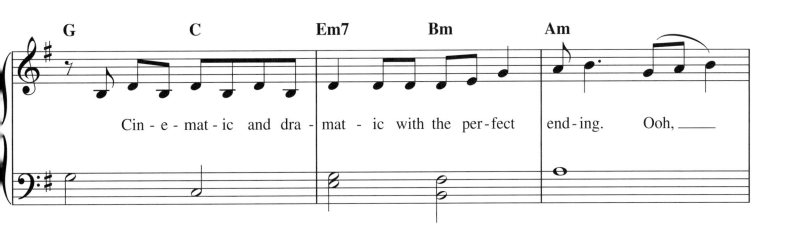

Cin - e - mat - ic and dra - mat - ic with the per - fect end - ing. Ooh, ___

it's not ___ like the mov - ies,

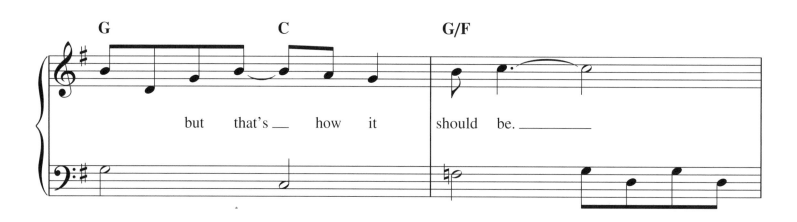

but that's ___ how it should be. _____

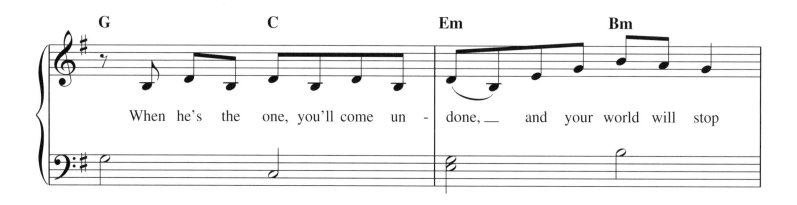

When he's the one, you'll come un - done, __ and your world will stop

spin - ing. And it's just the be - gin - ning.